JOB SEARCH SECRETS: A RECRUITER'S GUIDE TO LANDING YOUR DREAM JOB

Contents

"Job Search Secrets: A Recruiter's Guide to Landing Your Dream Job." offers thorough advice for job seekers at every step of their search by following this blueprint.

Introduction

Welcome Note

Welcome to "Job Search Secrets: A Recruiter's Guide to Landing Your Dream Job." Whether you are an experienced professional looking for a fresh challenge, a recent graduate starting your career, or someone returning to the industry, this book is meant to help you through every stage of the job hunt. With more than 20 years of recruitment experience, my name is Betty, and I have had the honor of assisting numerous people in securing their ideal employment.

I became Jake's professional coach when he was sick of applying for jobs repeatedly and never getting a call back. "We need to fix your resume, it is not attracting recruiters," I remember telling him. Upon analysis, Jake discovered a significant error on his resume that he had missed.

Madden was getting calls from recruiters and going to interviews, but she was getting dropped along the process. I then discovered that Madden had not done her homework on the firms she was interviewing with in order to prepare for the interview.

I hope to impart the knowledge and insights I've gathered to assist you succeed in your job hunt through this book.

The Book's Objective

It doesn't have to be difficult or burdensome to go through the job search process. This book's goal is to demystify the job search process while offering you useful, doable advice gleaned from my many years of hiring and choosing applicants. This book covers all the bases for landing the ideal job: being ready for the hunt, creating the ideal resume, slaying interviews, and negotiating offers. By the time this book ends, you will possess the abilities, know-how, and self-assurance required to make an impression on prospective employers and land the position you want.

Disclaimer:

The Value of a Well-Guided Job Search

A planned approach to job searching is more vital than ever in the competitive employment market of today. A well-planned strategy improves your chances of success by allowing you to concentrate your efforts and make efficient use of your time. Why a well-planned job search is essential is as follows:

Concentrated Efforts: Apply to particular positions and organizations that fit your talents and career objectives rather than just any company.

Efficiency: You can reduce the overwhelming and more manageable nature of the job search process by streamlining your efforts with a well-defined plan.

Making an Impression: You can position yourself as the best applicant for every opportunity by customizing your cover letter and resume for each application and thoroughly preparing for interviews.

Long-Term Success: By matching your duties with your career aspirations, a strategic job search not only helps you find a job but also puts you in a position for long-term professional progress and happiness.

Overview of the Book

This book is organized in ways to provide you with the information and abilities needed for a fruitful job search:

- Chapter 1: Getting Ready for the Job Search - read about the significance of self-evaluation, goal-setting, and creating a job search strategy.
- Chapter 2, "Crafting the Perfect Resume," you will learn what makes a resume stand out, how to customize it for a particular job, and typical pitfalls to avoid.
- Chapter 3, "Writing an Effective Cover Letter," you will learn the goal of the letter, how to format it, and how to make it more unique.
- Chapter 4, "Building an Online Presence," you will learn how to create a powerful personal brand, manage your online reputation, and optimize your LinkedIn profile.
- Chapter 5, Employing job boards, networking, and collaborating with recruiters are just a few of the efficient job search techniques covered in Job Search Strategies.
- Chapter 6: Ace the Interview: Get ready for various interview formats, typical interview questions, and useful strategies like the STAR method.
- Chapter 7: Following Up - teaches you how to follow up effectively, manage rejections in a positive way, and observe proper post-interview behavior.
- Chapter 8: Negotiating job offers- recognize how to evaluate a job offer, bargain for a better wage and perks, and reach a conclusion in a professional manner.

If you take the advice in this book to heart, you'll be ready to tackle your job hunt with confidence and strategy. Together, let's start this trip and get your job hunt off to a great start. You may attain your career objectives and land your dream job with the appropriate planning and approach.

Welcome to "Job Search Secrets: A Recruiter's Guide to Landing Your Dream Job " Now let's get going!

1

Getting Ready for the Job Hunt

Self-Evaluation: Determining Capabilities, Weaknesses, Interests, and Skills

Which path would you want to take in your career? What is your field of interest? This first stage will provide you a clear understanding of your interests, talents, shortcomings, and strengths, which will help you build a strong resume.

Determine Your Advantages and Disadvantages

Strengths: Consider your prior experiences, both personal and professional, to determine your strongest suit. Take into account the opinions of mentors, bosses, and coworkers. Consider this:

- Which tasks are fun and easy for me?
- What are the main things I've accomplished?
- For what abilities have I received consistent praise?

Weaknesses: It's equally critical to recognize your shortcomings. Acknowledge your areas of potential improvement and be sincere with yourself. Think about:

- Which tasks are difficult for me?

- Which are the skills I need to improve or lack?
- What criticism have I heard that identifies my areas of weakness?

My advice is always to lean into your areas of strength when deciding on your career.

Evaluate Your Capabilities

Technical skills are specialized, teachable abilities that you have gained by education or practical experience. Examples include technical equipment, programming languages, software, and software competency.

Soft skills are character traits including communication, teamwork, problem-solving, and time management that improve relationships, work output, and career opportunities.

Transferable skills are those that are applicable to different employment roles. Examples of these include analytical, project management, and leadership abilities. They are useful in many different sectors and occupations.

The skills you currently possess, combined with more you are willing to learn should be an important driver in choosing your career.

Establish Your Professional Goals

Short-term objectives are those you want to accomplish in the following one to two years. They ought to be precise and useful. As examples, consider:

- Gaining expertise in a specific field or position.
- Obtaining a certification or mastering a certain talent.
- Obtaining a specific role or title.

Long-term objectives are ones you want to accomplish within the next five to ten years. They ought to be in line with your long-term professional goals. As examples, consider:

- Gaining a position of leadership.
- Gaining proficiency in your area.
- Launching a consulting or business of your own.
- Time-limited: "I will complete the certification within the next 6 months."

Sync Your Objectives with Your Self-Evaluation

Make sure your objectives line up with the interests, talents, and qualities you discovered throughout the self-evaluation. This alignment will support you in maintaining your drive and concentration to meet your professional goals.

Here is the most important message for this Chapter. Once you have decided on a career path, TRY TO STAY FOCUSED. Many people will try to give you different sets of advice but you need to trust your self-evaluation and stay the course. You don't need to be talking to everyone but find one or two mentors in your chosen field to guide you along.

I have seen people hop from one field to the other with no clear path, wasting the precious time they could have spent focusing on one, developing themselves and growing. I am not in any way saying you cannot change careers but it cannot be too frequent.

Building your career in a specific field helps you to have deeper roots, become seasoned, and a master of that profession. We recruiters want to see consistency and growth in your career journey.

Creating a Job Search Plan: How to Develop a Successful Job Search Approach

Creating a thorough job search plan is the last stage in getting ready for your job search after you've completed your self-evaluation and set your goals. This strategy will operate as your road map, directing your activities and making sure you stay proactive and well-organized.

Investigate possible industries and employers, businesses and sectors that fit your interests, talents, and professional objectives. To learn more about possible employers, consult trade journals, professional networks, and internet resources.

Utilize Your Connection

Speak with people in your professional network for guidance, recommendations, and employment prospects. Join professional associations, go to industry events, and make connections with past coworkers and alumni.

Make Use of Company Websites and Online Job Boards

Check for fresh job advertisements on a regular basis on corporate websites and online job forums. To be updated about opportunities that are relevant to you, set up employment alerts.

Monitor Your Applications

Always check your emails. Recruiters will send interview invitations to more candidates than needed, this is because we don't want to be stuck if some don't respond. Providing your available times quickly helps us to get you on the hiring manager's calendar on time, and trust me these managers are very busy.

Note down the dates of your applications, the job descriptions, and your contact details for each position you apply for. This way when you get called and the name of the company gets mentioned, you have all their information handy to refer to. Remain organized and unwavering.

Get Ready for the Interview.

We will discuss this further in Chapter 6 "Ace the Interview"

It can take a while to get a job, but persistence and organization are key. Remain optimistic, take lessons from every encounter, and keep improving your strategy until you reach your objective.

You are developing a solid foundation for a successful job search by doing a complete self-evaluation, establishing specific goals, and creating an all-inclusive job search plan. Taking these first actions will help you remain motivated, organized, and focused, which will ultimately improve your chances of getting hired for the position that best suits your career goals.

We'll talk about creating the ideal resume in the upcoming chapter, one that effectively highlights your qualifications and makes an impression on prospective employers. Keep checking back and get set to advance in your career search!

2

Creating the Ideal resume

Can you guess how long it takes me to look through one resume?.................7 seconds! That's all it takes to decide whether or not your resume merits more review. Your key to getting an interview is having a strong resume. Your ability to advance in the employment process is greatly impacted by the first impression you give. I'll go over the principles of writing a resume that stands out in this chapter, as well as the significance of customizing it for each job application and typical errors to avert in order to make sure your resume is seen.

Adapting Your Resume: Making It Particular for Certain Job Applications

You'll find out from reading through certain job descriptions that a one size fits all resume may not be effective. Sometimes adapting your resume to specific job applications raises your chances of being spotted considerably. This is how you do it:

1. Determine the Core competencies: Examine the job description to determine the essential core competencies. Make sure these abilities are a major part of your prior positions on your resume.

2. Customize Your Experience: Edit your job descriptions to highlight responsibilities and achievements relevant to the role you're seeking.

3. Employ Keywords Specific to Your Industry: Filters are set in the applicant tracking system (ATS) by recruiters using keywords. For this reason, resumes without the keywords we've specified for a given job description are screened out, so you should include industry-specific terms from the job description in your resume. This makes it more likely that the recruiter will see your resume when it goes through applicant tracking systems (ATS).

4. Consistent Job Titles: If the title you previously had was exclusive to your organization but did not accurately describe your position, you might want to provide a more widely accepted title in parenthesis.

5. Display Career Development: If you've had comparable positions, describe your growth in each one. Emphasize leadership positions, growing responsibility, or specific abilities acquired through time.

6. Consistency: I have seen resumes that portray several different careers such as a teaching assistant, sales representative, and administrative assistant. Not beneficial... Showing recruiters that you are dedicated to a specific field by displaying a continuous career path towards the kind of position you are seeking gives them confidence.

7. Measure Your Success: Concentrate on quantifiable accomplishments that demonstrate your influence in related areas rather than just listing responsibilities. When feasible, quantify the impact of your contributions (e.g., "increased sales by 30%").

8. Customized Achievements: If you have a variety of relevant experiences, make sure that the accomplishments you include for each one align with the goals of the new position.

Resume Foundations: Essential Components of an Outstanding Resume

A strong resume is easy to read, highlights your experiences and qualifications that are pertinent to the position you're seeking for, and is clear and succinct. These are the essential components to have:

Details of Contact

Name: The resume should begin with your full name.

Phone: The main number to reach you.

Email address: One that is appropriate for business.

LinkedIn Profile: Provide a link to your current, professional LinkedIn profile.

Location: State and city (optional, but helpful for roles requiring a certain location).

Professional Summary

A clear description (three to five sentences) of your goals for the career, your strongest suit as an employee, and your main competencies.

Skills

A summary of your technical and soft skills that are relevant to the position you are applying for.

Employment History

Job Title: Position held.

Company Name: The organization's name.

Location: State and city.

Dates of Employment: Month and year of start and end.

Achievements and Responsibilities: List your achievements and responsibilities in bullet points. Pay attention to measurable outcomes (e.g., "Increased sales by 20%").

Education

Degree: Acquired degree.

Institution Name: The academic institution's name.

Location: State and city.

Date of Graduation: The graduation month and year.

Certifications and Training

List any completed training programs or certificates that are relevant to the position.

Experience volunteering (Optional)

Add any voluntary work that exhibits applicable abilities or backgrounds.

Common Errors to Avoid: Hazards That May Reduce the Impact of Your Resume

Preventing typical errors can have a big impact on how others view your resume. Here are a few things to watch out for:

Errors in grammar and spelling: This is a big NO! proofread your resume several times, and think about having a second set of eyes look it over. Negative impressions can be created by even little mistakes.

Making use of a non- professional email address: Make sure the email address you use is formal. Steer clear of nicknames or personal references that might not be taken seriously.

Including unrelated data: Pay attention to details that are pertinent to the position you are looking for. Remove experiences that are out of date or unnecessary if they don't bring value.

Employing a standard resume for every application: Customizing your resume becomes essential if you find that it does not fairly reflect the job description. Sometimes, a general resume may not highlight the particular abilities and experiences that an employer is seeking.

Absence of measurable results: Quantify your accomplishments whenever you can use figures, percentages, or precise results. This gives specific proof of your ability.

Variations in formatting: Keep your resume formatted in the same way the entire time. Make sure that headers and subheadings are consistent by using the same font style and size and aligning the bullet points.

Excessive length: Don't write a long resume. If you have fewer than ten years of experience, try to keep it to one page; if you have more experience, limit it to no more than two pages.

Neglecting to add keywords: If you leave out crucial keywords, the applicant tracking system may ignore your resume. Make sure your resume includes relevant keywords from the job description in a natural way.

Paying close attention to detail, having a clear grasp of your own experiences and qualifications, and being able to customize your application for each individual position are all necessary for creating the ideal resume. You can make your resume stand out to hiring managers and recruiters by adhering to the basics, including relevant keywords, and avoiding common blunders.

We will look at how to construct a strong cover letter that boosts your job application and works well with your resume in the next chapter. Remain concentrated as we continue to equip you with the resources you need to ace your job search!

3

How to Write a Strong Cover Letter

Once, I received a cover letter that grabbed my interest right away. The position was for a project manager at a computer company, and I had been going through a lot of applications that were all the same. However, this specific cover letter was unique from the outset.

"As a lifelong problem-solver, I found my calling in project management when I successfully led my first team in college to organize a charity event, raising over $8,000 in a single weekend," was the first personal narrative used to introduce the topic. This opening piqued my interest and demonstrated the candidate's initiative and commitment. I had the impression that I was getting to know the person behind the resume— exactly what a strong cover letter ought to accomplish.

The way they linked their individual experiences to the particular requirements of the business truly amazed me. They had obviously done their homework, citing one of the company's most recent product launches to demonstrate how their capacity to lead interdisciplinary teams and adhere to strict timelines would have made them ideal for the project. It was pertinent, straightforward, and tailored.

They told a story as opposed to a resume-style list of qualifications. They described how, at their previous employer, they had managed a team through a high-pressure product rollout, navigating unforeseen obstacles and managing budget and meeting all milestones. They discussed the outcomes of their work—increased efficiency and customer satisfaction ratings, for example—and discussed how they could succeed in this new position just as much.

By the end, I felt certain that this candidate genuinely wanted the position and understood the company's goals, so I wasn't only considering them based on their skills. Their enthusiasm and concise explanation of their potential contribution thrilled me to advance them in the procedure. It was the ideal illustration of the impact that a skillfully written cover letter can have.

An integral part of your job application is your cover letter. This is your chance to give a brief introduction, showcase your qualifications, and show that you are passionate about the position and the organization. A strong cover letter can have a big impact on whether hiring managers find your application noteworthy. I'll go over the goal of a cover letter, how to format and compose its text, and how to personalize it to leave a lasting impression in this chapter.

Why a Cover Letter Is Important and What It Should Aim to Achieve

Throughout the job application process, a cover letter fulfills a number of crucial functions.

Introduction: It gives the hiring manager a brief introduction to you and explains your background and motivation for applying for the position.

Emphasizing Qualifications: This feature enables you to draw attention to particular experiences and qualifications that set you apart as a competitive applicant for the job. This is your chance to demonstrate how your qualifications and experiences meet the needs of the position.

Exhibiting Enthusiasm: In your cover letter, you can share your excitement for the position and the business. It demonstrates that you have taken the time to learn about the organization's principles and objectives through research.

Taking Care of Any Gaps or Concerns: In your cover letter, you can succinctly and constructively address any gaps in your work history or any possible issues.

Motivating the Next Step: It acts as a prompt for the hiring manager to look over your resume and extend an invitation for a meeting.

Content and Structure: What to Include and How to Format

A cover letter that is well-structured is organized, succinct, and unambiguous. This is the suggested format:

Heading

Your Details for Contact: At the beginning of the cover letter, provide your name, address, phone number, and email address.
Date: Indicate the day the letter is being written.
Employer's Contact Information: Provide the hiring manager or employer's name, title, business name, and address.

Greetings

If at all feasible, address the letter to a particular individual. Instead of using a generic salutation like "To Whom It May Concern," use "Dear [Hiring Manager's Name]." You can use "Dear [Department] Team" or "Dear Hiring Committee" if you can't find the name.

Overview

Start with a compelling first sentence that catches the reader's interest. Give a brief introduction and mention the job for which you are applying. Explain how you learned about the employment opportunity and briefly discuss your reasons for being interested in the position and the organization.

Body Texts

First Paragraph: Emphasize your experiences and credentials that are most pertinent. Describe how your experience fits the job criteria and how you can help the business succeed.

Second Paragraph: Give particular instances from your experiences and accomplishments that highlight your abilities and credentials. Utilize measurable outcomes to increase influence. Talk about any special abilities or background that make you stand out from the competition.

Third Paragraph: Share your excitement for the position and the business. Describe your excitement for the opportunity and how it fits with the vision and culture of the organization, taking into account your values and career objectives.

Finishing

Reiterate your interest in the role and highlight your main points. Put a call to action in there, such as asking for an interview or saying you'll follow up. Express gratitude to the recruiting manager for their thought and time.

Add your signature

Finish with a formal phrase like "Sincerely" or "Best regards," then add your name. Make sure to leave room above your typed name for your signature if you are sending a physical letter.

Customization Advice: Creating a Unique Cover Letter

Your cover letter's efficacy can be greatly increased by personalizing it. The following advice will help your cover letter stand out:

Investigate the Company: Spend some time learning about the principles, ethos, and most recent successes of the organization. In order to demonstrate that you have done your research and that you are truly interested in the company, include particular data in your cover letter.

Adapt to the Job Description: Write a cover letter specifically for each application you submit. Emphasize your experiences and qualifications that are most applicable to the position for which you are seeking. To match the needs of the employer with your cover letter, use keywords found in the job description.

When addressing a cover letter, try to find out the recruiting manager's name and address it to them specifically. This kind gesture can leave a good impression.

Emphasize Your Special Value to differentiate yourself from the competition. Make sure to highlight your special abilities, noteworthy accomplishments, or relevant experiences that make you an asset to the team.

Be Sincere and Enthusiastic: Your cover letter should demonstrate your personality and excitement for the position. Steer clear of platitudes and generalizations. Rather, be sincere in expressing your interest in the role and the organization.

Keep It Brief: Try to keep your cover letter to no more than one page. Be succinct and direct, concentrating on the most crucial and pertinent details. Steer clear of needless information and drawn-out explanations.

Make sure your cover letter is devoid of typos, grammatical errors, and formatting problems by carefully proofreading it. Proofread it several times, and think about having a reliable friend or coworker check it as well. A strong cover letter can help you stand out from the competition and open doors, which will get you one step closer to getting the job of your dreams.

We will look at how to create a professional brand, manage your online reputation, enhance your LinkedIn profile, and have a strong online presence in the upcoming chapter. Together, let's keep moving forward to master your job search!

4

Establishing Your Online Identity

In my role as a recruiter, I regularly use the internet to research possible prospects. For instance, I perform cold searches on LinkedIn. Finding and interacting with possible applicants who might not have responded directly to a job posting is the aim.

I begin by focusing on job titles that are relevant to the position I'm hiring for. I also utilize relevant keywords (such as "Java Developer," "Product Manager," or "Sales Executive") that explain the necessary abilities or knowledge.

I then use a location filter to identify applicants who live in the relevant geographic area for the position or who have shown a desire to work remotely or relocate.

Lastly, I use filters based on years of experience to limit the pool of candidates to those who satisfy the seniority requirements for the position.

Your internet presence is an essential part of your job search strategy in the modern digital age. As a result, you can greatly improve your career prospects by maintaining your social media accounts, creating a strong personal brand, and improving your LinkedIn profile. We shall examine how to do this in this chapter.

Developing an Eye-Catching LinkedIn Profile through LinkedIn Optimization

Since LinkedIn is the most popular platform for professional networking, job seekers should not be without it. Here's how to make the most of your LinkedIn profile to draw in companies and recruiters:

Profile Image

Make use of a well-taken, expert photo. You should be dressed correctly for your industry and have your face prominently displayed.

Headline

Create a catchy headline that doesn't only mention your position. Make use of keywords that are relevant to your line of work and expertise. For instance, rather than just saying "Marketing Specialist," use "Marketing Specialist | SEO Expert | Content Creator."

Summary

Provide an engaging summary that emphasizes your experience in the field, your core competencies, and your future goals. For a more friendly and intimate tone, use the first-person narrative.

Experience

Put your professional background in reverse chronological order with the most recent job at the top. Provide a brief overview of your duties for each position and, if it's feasible, use quantitative data to emphasize your most significant accomplishments. For easier reading, use bullet points.

Skills and Endorsements

Make a list of your pertinent abilities and ask coworkers and superiors for recommendations. Give people in your network your endorsement as well; chances are they'll give it back.

Recommendations

Consult with clients, bosses, and former and current coworkers for recommendations. Sincere recommendations can give your profile more legitimacy.

Education

Provide a summary of your school history and any applicable degrees, courses, or professional development opportunities.

Participation

Join relevant groups, share articles, and leave comments on other people's postings to get involved on LinkedIn. This will show that you are involved in your field and raise your profile.

Details of Contact

Make sure your contact details are current and simple to find. Add your email address and any other pertinent information about yourself.

Social Media: Taking Charge of Your Online Image

Your presence on other social media sites, in addition to LinkedIn, may have an effect on your job hunt. The following advice can help you maintain your online reputation:

Examine the accounts you have on social networking sites such as Instagram, Twitter, and Facebook. Make sure the stuff you write presents a credible image. Any posts or images that can be interpreted as amateurish should be removed or hidden. Some company recruiters look at these.

Configurations for Privacy

You can manage who can view your posts and personal data by adjusting your privacy settings. Take care of what you disclose in public.

Regularity

Make sure that the personal and professional information on all of your social media platforms is consistent. Make sure your profile image, bio, and other information are all in alignment.

Use LinkedIn to interact with business people, join groups, and take part in conversations. You may be able to find work prospects and grow your network in this way.

Building and Sustaining a Professional Online Presence through Personal Branding

The way you show yourself to the business world is your personal brand. It's a culmination of your abilities, encounters, principles, and communication style. Here's how to develop and keep up a powerful personal brand:

Create a Brand Message

Create a clear and unambiguous brand message that expresses your identity, mission, and values. Your social network bios, LinkedIn summary, and other professional pages should all convey the same idea.

Interact with the People in Your Audience

Interact with your audience by leaving comments, joining in conversations, and establishing professional connections. Building relationships and increasing your visibility are two benefits of this contact.

Authenticity and Consistency

Make sure that your online persona is the same on all of the sites. In both your interactions and content, be genuine. Credibility and trust are increased by authenticity.

Having a strong online presence might help you stand out in the competitive job market and lead to new chances.

We will explore successful job search techniques, such as utilizing job boards, networking, and collaborating with recruiters, in the upcoming chapter. Together, let's keep moving forward to master your job search!

5

Techniques for Job Searching

We'll look at three essential elements of a successful job search in this chapter: making the most of networking opportunities, using online job boards and applications, and collaborating with recruiters and staffing agencies efficiently. Every one of these tactics is essential to assisting you in locating and landing the ideal employment.

Job Search Engine Optimization for Job Boards and Online Applications

Online applications and job boards are two of the most popular resources for job seekers. Here's how to make good use of them:

Selecting Appropriate Job Boards

General Job Boards: A variety of job advertisements across numerous industries can be found on websites such as Indeed, Monster, Glassdoor, and Zip Recruiter. These serve as excellent places for most job seekers to start.

Industry-Specific Job Boards: These job boards may be more helpful to you in your line of work. For instance, Hcareers is for the hospitality industry, Mediabistro is for media and communications, and Dice is for computer employment.

Career Pages for Companies: A lot of businesses post job openings on their own websites. Check the career pages of the companies you are considering on a regular basis.

Making Alerts for Jobs

To get notified when new job posts that fit your criteria are posted, set up job alerts on the employment forums of your choice. By doing this, you can avoid continuously searching for chances and stay up to date on relevant ones.

Making the Most of Your Network to Find Jobs

Notify Your Network: Share your employment search with those you know. Be clear about the kind of position you're looking for.

Request Referrals: Seek referrals from people in your network who are employed by a company that interests you, in order to be considered for a job opening.

Staffing Agencies and Recruiters: How to Collaborate with Recruiters

Insights into the recruiting process and access to unadvertised vacancies make recruiters and staffing agencies invaluable allies in your job quest.

Recognizing Various Recruiter Types

Internal Recruiters: These recruiters fill openings within an organization directly on behalf of the employer.

External Recruiters: Often referred to as headhunters or staffing agencies, these recruiters search for qualified applicants for job openings on behalf of numerous client companies.

Temporary Staffing Agencies: These organizations place applicants in contract or temporary jobs, some of which may eventually lead to permanent ones.

Selecting the Appropriate Recruiter

Find staffing companies or recruiters who specialize in your sector or field by doing some research. Seek out respectable organizations with a solid track record and glowing testimonials.

We will discuss how to ace the interview process in the upcoming chapter, along with advice on how to use behavioral interview methods, answer typical interview questions, and prepare for various interview scenarios. Together, let's keep moving forward to master your job search!

6

Ace the Interview

The interview stage is the one that interests me the most as a recruiter. Here's where I get to meet the people behind the names on the resume and get to know their personalities. Have you ever wondered why hiring managers can't just look at your professionally written resume and accept you? Not so quickly:)

Technical accomplishments and talents can be listed on a resume, but during an interview, we can judge a candidate's capacity for meaningful chats, clear thinking, and good communication—all of which are important abilities for many positions. It's hard to adequately convey on a resume how well a candidate fits in with the team dynamics, corporate culture, and values, but interviews offer an opportunity to find out.

I always advise my mentees to stand in front of a mirror and practice with their resume. This helps you to manage your facial and body expressions to exude confidence. Even though we recruiters and hiring managers have read your resume, we need to hear you flow well on your career journey. The excitement you show in sharing your prior experiences and accomplishments rubs off on us. We can always tell candidates who have practiced because they are able to articulate their words better, turning their resume into a career story. Study frequently asked interview questions and rehearse your answers. Make a list of inquiries you want to make of the interviewer regarding the position and business.

The Effective Interview

I recall one interview in which everything fell into place. The candidate was eager, engaging, and well-prepared from the outset of our interview process for the associate marketing manager position. She had obviously done her homework on the business, citing particular initiatives that we had undertaken and talking about how she could offer fresh insights.

She didn't merely provide a vague answer when I asked her about a difficult assignment she had overseen. Rather, she took me through every step of the process, from the planning stage to the execution, the obstacles they faced, and the way her team made last-minute strategy adjustments. She emphasized quantifiable results, such as a 25% increase in engagement and fulfilling all deadlines in spite of obstacles.

Her ability to listen and then intelligently react, making a direct connection between her experience and what we were seeking for in the role, was what impressed us the most. She demonstrated real curiosity in learning how she could contribute to the company's progress by asking perceptive questions regarding its future objectives. At the conclusion of the interview, I was certain that she was a fantastic fit for the team in addition to being qualified.

The Unsatisfactory Interview

However, the interview I had for a senior sales position was entirely different. I was excited to meet the candidate since their resume caught my attention. But it was obvious right away that they had not prepared. They found it difficult to describe their prior positions and frequently responded with brief, vague explanations that offered little insight into their backgrounds.

They were unable to recollect any specifics or metrics when asked about a period when they had met a difficult sales objective, and their response was evasive and unpersuasive. Even worse, they gave off the impression that they were eager for the interview to end because they seldom made eye contact and frequently looked at their watches. They showed no genuine interest in the position or the organization, as seen by their lack of queries.

By the end of the interview, it was obvious that although their resume looked perfect, it was hard to proceed with them due to their lack of excitement, preparation, and ability to clearly communicate their experience. It served as a helpful reminder that interview appearance is just as important as having a stellar resume.

Interviews are an essential part of the job search process since they provide you the chance to show off your credentials, abilities, and suitability for the position. This chapter will cover a variety of interview topics, including frequent interview questions, preparation advice, and behavioral interviewing strategies.

Interview types include in-person, video, and phone interviews.

It can be helpful to know the many kinds of interviews so that you can prepare for each scenario.

Telephone Interviews

Goal: Frequently used as a preliminary screening to see if you fulfill the fundamental qualifications for the position.

Advice: Speak clearly, make sure you're in a calm place, and have your resume and job description in front of you. Make sure your tone is clear and succinct. It helps if you can stay standing while talking, this enhances your voice.

Video-Based Interviews

Goal: Becoming more widespread, particularly for remote jobs or initial rounds of interviews.

Advice: Make sure your lighting is adequate, test your equipment beforehand, pick a formal backdrop, and dress accordingly. Keep your gaze on the camera rather than the screen to maintain eye contact.

Personal Interviews

Goal: Usually used to determine how well you fit into the team and culture of the business in the last phases of the hiring process.

Advice: Dress formally, present yourself properly, bring several copies of your resume, and be ready to strike up a conversation to start a conversation.

Panel Discussions

Goal: Has several interviewers from various departments evaluate your credentials at the same time.

Advice: Use proper salutations, look each panelist in the eye, and be ready for a range of questions.

Researching the Company and Role in Advance

Mission and Values: Recognize the goals, principles, and culture of the organization. This enables you to modify your responses so that they meet their priorities.

Products and Services: Be aware of the company's offerings, target market, and any new information or advancements.

Position in the Industry: Educate yourself on the issues, trends, and rivals facing the sector.

Practice Answering Questions

Possible Questions: Prepare responses that showcase your experiences and talents in anticipation of questions based on the job description.

Practice Typical Questions: Prepare responses to frequently asked interview questions (refer to the section below).

Prepare the interviewer's questions: Prepare some intelligent questions regarding the role, team, and company to ask the interviewer.

Organizational logistics

Time and Place: Verify the specifics of the interview, such as the time, place, and names of your interviewers. Do not be late! Lateness is a major knock out for candidates, no matter how good the profile is.

Supplies: Bring a notepad, a pen, several copies of your resume, and a list of references.

Frequently Asked Questions

When Asked, Tell Me About Yourself, Please

Advice: Give a simple rundown of your work history, emphasizing significant accomplishments and pertinent encounters. Remain succinct and career-focused.

What Attracts You to This Job?

Advice: Show off your familiarity with the business and show that you are really excited about the position and how it fits into your career objectives.

What Are Your Strengths and Weaknesses?

Emphasize your strengths that are pertinent to the position. When talking about your weaknesses, emphasize your progress and the lessons you've learnt.

Explain a Difficult Situation and How You Solved It.

Advice: To explain the scenario, task, action, and outcome, use the STAR approach (see below). Stress your resilience and problem-solving abilities.

In five years, where do you see yourself?

Advice: Be aspirational and supportive of the expansion of the business. Pay attention to how you want to advance your career and how you can help the organization.

Why Should We Employ You?

Advice: List your main skills and how they meet the needs of the position. Emphasize your special qualities and the ways in which you may benefit the team.

Are You Asking Us Any Questions?

Advice: Yes, you must ask questions. Make perceptive inquiries on the company's growth prospects, team dynamics, and culture. This shows that you are involved and interested.

Techniques for Behavioral Interviewing: The STAR Method and Other Approaches

Behavioral interview questions gauge your past behavior to forecast your future actions.

STAR Approach

Situation: Explain the environment in which you overcame an obstacle or completed an activity.

Task: Describe the assignment you were in charge of.

Action: Specify the precise steps you followed to complete the assignment.

Result: Discuss the conclusions or effects of your activities, emphasizing your accomplishments.

For example, a recruiter asks a candidate seeking a HR Manager role this question:

"Can you tell me about a time when you handled, or participated in a work project?"

Here, recruiters want a detailed example of a situation. First, we expect you to present a specific situation or an important need, second, the task or assignment to be completed, third, the action you took, and lastly, the result (always use examples that ended with success).

Many candidates fail to give specific examples. Instead, giving vague answers like "during projects, we usually create a task force to handle implementations........." already knocks a candidate out. So, I am not even going to continue typing this example :)

As opposed to a candidate who says "I remember last year when my company needed to implement a new HR software because the old one was outdated, we hired consultants to help us with creating a new platform to support all our HR modules, as the HR Coordinator, my role was to clean up the current employee data, making sure that all employee information, like dates, addresses, and document uploads were correct. I even took the opportunity to gather education level information from employees (which we did not have in the outgoing system). Once this exercise was complete, I provided the template to our consultants for upload into the new system. The project turned out to be a big success which brought about a 25% reduction to HR data entry time. See the difference? :)

Exercise

Mock Interviews: Practice your responses and get feedback by holding mock interviews with a friend or mentor.

You may go into every interview with confidence if you know what to expect, how to prepare well, practice frequently asked interview questions, and become an expert in behavioral interviewing strategies. Getting the job you want requires you to perform well in the interview.

We will discuss the significance of following up following an interview in the upcoming chapter, along with follow-up techniques, thank-you notes, and how to handle rejections. Together, let's keep moving forward to master your job search!

7

Concluding

I'm always struck by candidates who follow up with thank-you notes following the interview. I recall our interview for a logistics manager position at a manufacturing company where I was previously employed. After two outstanding candidate interviews, our panel of four interviewers was having trouble selecting which of the two qualified prospects to extend the offer to during the debriefing. While we were still talking, I received a notification via email. It was one of the two applicants who had thanked me and asked me to extend their appreciation to the hiring manager. I informed him and right there and then, the hiring manager responded, "that's the one I am going with!!" Maintaining momentum in your job hunt and leaving a lasting impression depend on how well you handle the post-interview period. This chapter will cover how to handle rejections politely, follow up with effectiveness, and post-interview etiquette.

Following an Interview: Writing a Thank-You Note

After an interview, sending a thank-you note is an easy yet effective approach to express gratitude and reaffirm your interest in the job.

Reasons to Write Thank-You Notes

- Expresses gratitude: Writing a thank-you note expresses appreciation for the interviewer's time and thought.

- Reiterates Interest: It reaffirms your excitement for the position and business.

- Maintains Your Presence: It offers a chance to make a good, long-lasting impression.

- When within 24 hours of the interview, you send your word of appreciation, it demonstrates zeal and promptness.

Structure of thank you message

Email: The most popular and efficient way is email. Make sure your email is error-free and written properly.

Say hello and use the interviewer's name, express your gratitude to the interviewer for the chance and their time, add a personal touch by mentioning a particular subject or idea that stuck out to you from the interview, reiterate Interest: State again how excited you are about the position and why you think you'd be a good fit and finally, conclude in a formal manner.

For instance:

Dear [Name of Interviewee],

I appreciate your time yesterday. I was genuinely grateful for the chance to find out more about [Company Name] and the [Job Title] role.

Hearing about [particular issue mentioned] particularly thrilled me and reaffirmed my excitement for the position. I'm sure that my experience with [relevant experience] and [particular talent] make me a great addition to your team.

I'm enthusiastic to apply my [particular quality] to the role and am excited about the prospect of working with [Company Name]. Kindly do not hesitate to contact us in case you require any additional details.

Again, I appreciate your time and thoughtfulness.

Warm regards,

[Name]

Follow-Up Techniques: When and How to Continue the Conversation After an Interview

Staying involved in the hiring process might be facilitated by following up after the initial thank-you note.

Initial Follow-Up: One week following your thank-you note, send a courteous follow-up email if you haven't heard back within the timeframe that was mentioned during the interview.

Follow-Ups Afterwards: If no time frame was specified, follow up every two weeks. Aim for no more than two follow-ups to avoid coming across as aggressive.

For instance:

Dear [Name of Interviewee],

I hope you are doing well as I write this. I had an interview on [date] for the [Job Title] position, and I'm writing to inquire about the status of my application. The chance to work with [Company Name] and add value to your team excites me much.

Would you please let me know if there have been any developments with my application? Kindly notify me if I may offer any more details or if there are any further steps in the procedure that need to be completed.

Again, I appreciate your time and thoughtfulness.

Warm regards,

[Name]

Managing Rejections: Converting a "No" into an Educational Opportunity

The job search procedure will inevitably result in rejections. Taking care of them properly can help you succeed in the future.

Reacting to Rejections

Express gratitude to the employer: Thank them for their consideration and the chance.

Request input: To identify areas that need work, kindly ask for input.

Remain Professional: Keep your demeanor upbeat and professional while remaining open to new opportunities.

For instance:

Dear [Name of Interviewee],

I appreciate you letting me know about your choice for the [Job Title] post. I really appreciate the chance to interview with [Company Name], even though I am unhappy that I was not chosen.

I would appreciate any input you could have regarding my performance in the interview or on my application. It would be really helpful to understand your viewpoint as I look for chances in this industry.

Again, I appreciate your time and thoughtfulness. I'm hoping to get the opportunity to apply for any upcoming positions at [Company Name].

Warm regards,

[Name]

Gaining Knowledge from Recommendations

Examine the Comments: Give careful thought to any criticism you've received and note any areas that need work.

Seek Patterns: To identify persistent areas of weakness, look for recurring themes in the comments from various interviewees.

Sustaining Happiness

Rejections shouldn't define you or your potential. Remain resilient. Remain strong and have an optimistic attitude.

Concentrate on Your Growth: See every setback as a chance to get better. Each interview is an educational opportunity that advances your objective.

Extend Your Search: Think about extending your search to encompass other roles or industries as you reassess your job search approach.

We will discuss negotiating employment offers in the upcoming chapter, along with how to comprehend their components, how to negotiate salary, and how to properly accept offers. Together, let's keep moving forward to master your job search!

8

Understanding Job Offers

Let's take a brief detour before discussing offers. Have you ever been asked about what pay you are seeking for by a recruiter? And you go with the safest way to respond, "able to negotiate," hoping that the recruiter will name his or her price/range but instead, the recruiter insists you provide them with an amount? Don't be caught unaware!

Recruiters are curious for the following straightforward reason. A predetermined range of funds has previously been budgeted for each job. Most businesses may have done a compensation exercise prior to budgeting, which enables them to assess each position, compare salaries across markets, and ultimately determine a pay range for each position. I may be oversimplifying, but it's a demanding task that can take months at times.

Therefore, even though we like your resume, we must confirm that your pay requirements are within the specified ranges. Like the majority of recruiters, I typically pose these questions during the first phone screen. I want to make sure I'm not wasting either of our time at this early point. You will learn more on doing salary research later in this chapter.

Comprehending the Offer: Dissecting the Elements of a Job Offer

Receiving a job offer represents a noteworthy achievement in your pursuit of employment. To make sure you receive the greatest conditions and get started in your new work straight away, it's important to comprehend the offer, negotiate your compensation, and accept the offer effectively.

However, there are more details involved in a job offer than just the pay. Comprehending every component will enable you to assess the offer in its whole.

Pay

- Base Salary: Your set hourly, monthly, or yearly compensation.
- Bonuses: Annual or performance-based bonuses can greatly increase your overall salary, but they are not guaranteed.

Benefits

- Health Insurance: Plans provided by the employer for medical, dental, and vision care. Examine the costs and details of the coverage.
- Retirement Plans: employer-matched contributions, 401(k) plans, and other retirement savings choices.
- Paid Time Off (PTO) includes holidays, sick days, and vacation time. Recognize the constraints and the accrual process.
- Work schedule: Regular work schedule with overtime obligations.
- Remote Work: Possibilities for working remotely or with flexible hours.
- Advancement of the Profession
- Training and Education: Possibilities for more coursework, credentials, or training courses.

Extra Benefits

- Equity options are chances to buy business equity at a reduced price.

- Wellness Programs: Availability of fitness centers, wellness initiatives, and other health-related advantages.

- Assistance with Relocation: Financial support for relocation costs in the event that you must move for work.

Tips for Salary Negotiation: How to Ask for More Money and Benefits

Although it can be scary, negotiating your pay and perks is a necessary skill to make sure you're paid fairly

When you are asked the golden question of "what salary are you looking for? "If you answer with "negotiable" and the recruiter accepts, you may have to wait till they give you the offer letter and then determine if you are satisfied based on your research or if you want to negotiate further.

However, the scenario to discuss pay before you receive the offer letter may happen if the recruiter insists that you should name your salary range during the interviews, so do some research and get ready!

Also, remember you do not have to mention your current pay. In fact, as of today, several states in the U.S. have laws in place that prevent employers and recruiters from asking about salary history. Some recruiters may take the advantage of knowing your current lower pay to offer you less.

How to Conduct Salary Research

Market Rates: Use resources like Glassdoor, PayScale, and industry reports to research industry standards and salary ranges for your role and experience level.

For example, if I am seeking an HR Manager job and live in Houston TX, I will type in google search "Glassdoor HR Manager Houston, TX Salary for ……. (enter the name of the company).

So, let's say you get a range of $87,000 -$156,000 per year for that company (again, this is just an example)

Determine the midpoint, in this case, it will be at around **$120,000.**

Next, factor your total years of experience in that field. (experience in other fields may not count)

Scenario 1: If you have junior level experience e.g. 1 - 3 years, stay closer to the beginning of the range. My response in this case will be, "based upon my research and experience, for this job, I will consider between $90,000 - $120,000" (making the midpoint 120k the end of your range)

Scenario 2: Still using the HR Manager example, if you have mid- level experience e.g. 4 -7 years, move to the middle of the range. My response in this case will be, "based upon my research and experience, for this job, I will consider between $120,000 - $140,000" (making the 120k midpoint the beginning of your range).

Scenario 3: If you have senior level experience e.g. 8 -10 years, go closer to the end of the range. My response in this case will be, "based upon my research and experience, for this job, I will consider between $140,000 - $156,000".

Along with stating your pay range, highlight the special abilities, background, and accomplishments that sets you apart from the competition.

Then end with **"can you let me know what your company's pay range for this job is?"** At this point, the recruiter will be very inclined to give you an answer, then you can determine if what they are offering aligns with your own salary needs.

Please remember that each company decides where pay will fall along general market rates. Industry, size, financial standing and location are big factors that determine how well a company will pay.

For example, if this HR Manager candidate was applying to a tech company, there is more probability that they will offer higher pay along these ranges than if it was a manufacturing company.

When to Start a Negotiation

Following the Offer: Negotiate only after you've received a formal job offer (verbal or letter). This indicates that the employer is considering hiring you already.

Examine the Offer: Before talking about any adjustments, take your time going over the offer in its entirety. This demonstrates that you're thinking about more than just your pay.

Effective Communication

Act with professionalism: Treat the negotiation with decency and professionalism. Refrain from issuing commands or warnings.

Be Particular: Express your desired pay or perks in clear terms. If you're willing to compromise but have a specific budget in mind, give a range.

Justify Your Request: Provide evidence of your accomplishments and own research to support your request for a higher pay or better benefits.

Think About the Entire Package

Trade-offs: Be prepared to give up certain benefits in exchange for your pay. If a greater pay isn't an option, try negotiating for extra vacation time or chances for professional growth.

Get Your Pitch in Order

Role-play: To gain confidence and get feedback, practice your bargaining pitch with a friend or mentor. Overall, remain calm and confident. Recognize that negotiations are a normal part of the recruiting process and approach the conversation with a confident demeanor.

Accepting the Offer: Choosing a Course of Action and Reacting Correctly

It's time to take the offer and start the next chapter of your career once you've negotiated the greatest conditions.

Consider the Final Offer

Total Compensation: Take into account the earnings package as a whole, which includes salary, benefits, and extra incentives.

Career Objectives: Evaluate how the position fits with your long-term professional development and career objectives.

Work-Life Balance: Verify if the position accommodates your personal obligations and desired work-life balance.

Official Recognition

Written Acceptance: Acknowledge the employment offer in writing, in an official manner. This could be a signed offer letter or an email, then thank the employer for the chance and let them know how excited you are to be a part of the team.

For instance:

Dear [Name of Hiring Manager],

It gives me great pleasure to accept the offer from [Company Name] for the [Job Title] position. I appreciate the chance, and I'm eager to help the team and the business succeed.

After going over the specifics of the offer, I'm happy with the entire compensation package. If there are any more processes or papers I need to provide before my start date on [Start Date], do let me know.

Again, I want to thank you for this chance. Working with you and the rest of the team is something I'm excited about.

Warm regards,

[Name]

Notifying Additional Employers

Notify Other Prospects: Let them know that you've decided to accept another offer if you were in talks with any other prospective employers. Remain professional and keep the door open for other chances.

For instance:

Dear [Name of Hiring Manager],

For the [Job Title] position at [Company Name], I wanted to express my gratitude for your consideration of my application. I've made the decision to accept another offer that closely fits with my career aspirations after giving it some thought.

I value the time and work you put into our conversations, and I hope to cross your way again in the future.

Warm regards,

[Name]

Get Ready for your move

Current Employer: If you are still working, give your employer a written letter of resignation and follow the notice period outlined in your employment agreement.

Onboarding Readiness: Start getting ready for your new position by being acquainted with the company's onboarding procedure and any relevant resources.

Through comprehension of the elements included in a job offer, skillful negotiation of pay and benefits, and a professional acceptance of the offer, you can land a job that fulfills your requirements and positions you for success. To guarantee a seamless transition into your new career and foster a good working relationship with your new employer, each stage in this process is crucial.

You are prepared to handle the job hunt from beginning to end with these abilities and tactics. Well done on making it to this point, and good luck with your new profession!

Conclusion
Last Words of Wisdom

As you start your job hunt, keep in mind that perseverance and an optimistic outlook are essential. Although the process can be difficult, every step you take will get you closer to your destination. Here are a few last words of wisdom:

Rejections and obstacles are inevitable on the path; remain resilient. Seize the chance to develop and learn from them.

Engage in Active Networking: Creating and sustaining business connections might lead to new prospects.

Continue Learning: To stay competitive, keep up with industry developments and work to enhance your skills on a constant basis.

Be Genuine: Throughout the job search process, stay loyal to who you are and your principles. Genuineness will appeal to the appropriate employers.

Materials

These are some excellent tools to help you in your job search:

- Websites for Job Searches
- Visit LinkedIn at www.linkedin.com.
- True: https://www.true.com
- Glassdoor: https://www.glassdoor.com
- Monster can be found online.
- https://www.canva.com
- Zety: www.zety.com
- Office Templates from Microsoft: templates.office.com

Advancement of the Profession

Visit Coursera at www.coursera.org.

LinkedIn Education: https://www.linkedin.com/education

https://www.udemy.com/

Visit Eventbrite at www.eventbrite.com.

Professional Associations: Look up associations in your area for resources and networking opportunities.

Through the use of these tools and the tactics described in this book, you will be well-equipped to move through the job search process with assurance and efficiency. Recall that your dream job exists, and you can locate it with the correct strategy and persistence.

I wish you well with your upcoming career pursuits and job search!

We appreciate you taking the time to read "Job Search Secrets: A Recruiter's Guide to Landing Your Ideal Job." I hope this book has given you insightful knowledge and useful advice to help you reach your professional objectives. Continue to be resolute and optimistic, and succeed in your job search!

Glossary

Applicant Tracking System (ATS): A software application used by employers to manage the recruiting process, including posting job openings and screening resumes.

Behavioral Interview: An interview technique where the interviewer asks candidates to provide examples of past experiences that demonstrate specific skills or behaviors.

Branding: The process of creating a unique image or identity for oneself in the job market, often through a personal brand that reflects skills, values, and career goals.

Career Objective: A brief statement on a resume that outlines the candidate's career goals and what they aim to achieve in their professional life.

Cover Letter: A document sent with a resume to provide additional information on a candidate's skills and experience. It typically explains why the candidate is interested in the position and how they are a good fit.

Job Description: A detailed outline of the responsibilities, requirements, and expectations for a specific role within a company.

Keywords: Specific words or phrases used in resumes and cover letters to match the language of the job description. These are often used by ATS to screen resumes.

LinkedIn: A professional networking platform used to connect with colleagues, showcase skills and experience, and search for job opportunities.

Mentorship: A professional relationship in which an experienced individual (mentor) provides guidance, advice, and support to a less experienced person (mentee).

Networking: Building and maintaining professional relationships that can provide job leads, advice, or support during a job search.

Offer Letter: A formal letter from an employer to a candidate outlining the terms and conditions of employment.

Passive Candidate: A candidate who is not actively looking for a job but may be open to new opportunities if approached by a recruiter.

Personal Branding: The practice of marketing oneself and one's career as a brand, using social media, personal websites, and other tools to showcase skills and expertise.

Recruiter: A professional who specializes in finding and hiring candidates for job openings within an organization or for clients.

Reference: A person who can provide a testimonial about a candidate's skills, experience, and work ethic, usually contacted during the final stages of the hiring process.

Resume: A formal document that summarizes a candidate's work experience, education, skills, and accomplishments, used to apply for jobs.

Soft Skills: Interpersonal and personal skills that are not specific to any job but are essential for success in the workplace, such as communication, teamwork, and problem-solving.

Transferable Skills: Skills gained from past experiences that are applicable to a wide range of jobs and industries, such as communication, leadership, and analytical thinking.

Virtual Interview: A job interview conducted remotely via video conferencing tools, often used in the initial stages of the hiring process or for remote positions.

Work-Life Balance: The equilibrium between personal life and career work, emphasizing the importance of both in maintaining overall well-being and job satisfaction.